ABSTRACT

EMOTIONS THAT SHOULD BE PAINTED, BUT ARE WRITTEN

FELEREEN ADORISA
TARIANG

Made with ♥ on the Notion Press Platform
www.notionpress.com

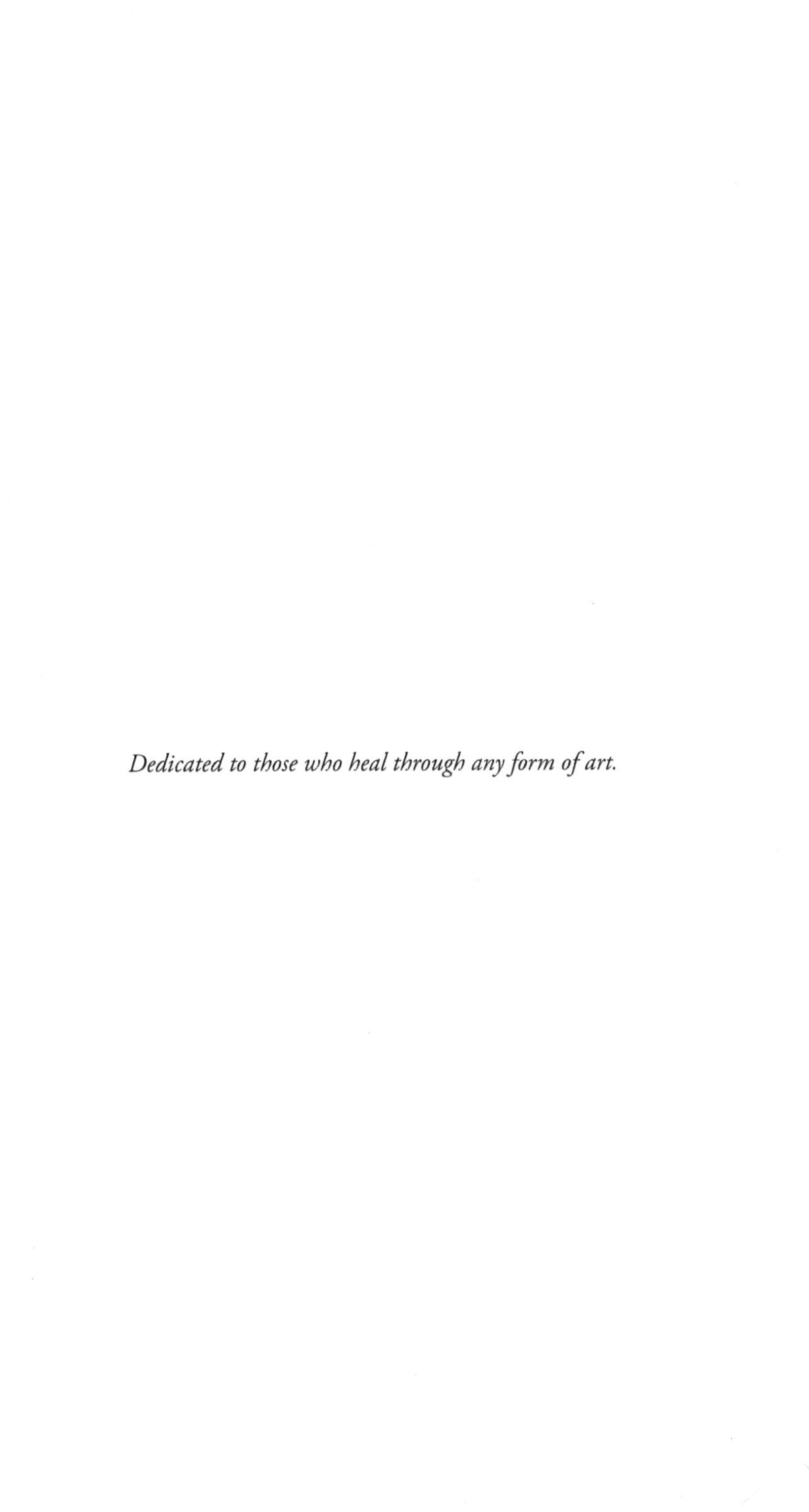

Dedicated to those who heal through any form of art.

Contents

Contents

Preface

A painted Preface by Felereen Adorisa Tariang

I decided to frame my emotions in the form of poetry. Some would be able to resonate and re-live their own personal emotions and some would be delving into the museum of my mind, and find out who I truly am, which baffles me too, at times.

Acknowledgements

I am grateful to God for the gift of translating emotions into art and more so, in my case, poetry. I would like to honour my parents who have been my best friends and my biggest supporters even in times when I could not like myself. I would like to thank my sister for being my inspiration and for having read all my poems with honest feedbacks. With all my heart, I would also like to honour my Grandpa for always making me feel like the luckiest granddaughter in the whole wide world. A heartfelt gratitude to whoever is making time to read this little work of mine, I wish you the best in everything that you do. Most importantly, I would like to give all the glory to my God and Saviour, Jesus Christ, for without Him, I am nothing.

1. Madness

This madness is not a noun,
Nor your cliché kind of craziness;
This madness wears a smile,
Sometimes it is half crooked and
Sometimes it is wild.
This madness has a heart;
Whose lubb dubb sound only echoes for one,
This madness is in love,
And to her, she has found the one.
This madness had never shown pain,
For to everyone, she is full of zest!
Her lover though, whom she adores,
Finds her in her mess and gives her his best;
However, to him, she only comes off as madness.
The concealed heartaches are shown to him,
Her chaotic mind is being felt by him,
She loves him dearly, yet she burst into flames
At the sight and sound of minor errs;
Followed by tears and deep regrets!
She hurts the one she loves the most
Because she is madness.
With words she never used, she speaks;
Inspite of him being

The only one that she would seek.
Is this madness too in love?
Or is she just madness?
Amid the chaos,
She thinks of him,
The one who finds her in broken pieces;
"Is he alright? Will he be fine?"
She hates herself for she has to see:
What her lover has to endure to eternity
For falling in love with madness.

2. The story of a cool, uncool yet very cool boy

I almost tripped, but I had a strong grip,
I was told not to let blasé words ruin the trip.
They raised me well, even my finest companion could tell;
But environment turned that finesse into a living hell.
And then I started hating rules,
And thought that smoking pot was something cool.
I wore a facade to please my kin,
And homeless I would be, had they checked my bin.
How dreadfully funny their faces would be
To see me high on New Year's eve.
But, that never ought to be,
For in my life, I never got a B!
Was drenched and tried to quench my thirst,
While I read about the universe;
For traffic made me so thirsty,
It was then that they told me
That I would soon get a college degree.
Maturity had struck me hard,
That I dreaded to even dream about the past.
I was lucky to have never been caught,
For the constant straight A's were my cloak.
I saw things differently then,

I became a perfect ten;
For I realized that life did not turn its back on me
Even while I was smoking weed.
I now recall each interesting moment,
The highs, the falls and the extraordinary achievements.
I look back to the uncool days
And shyly laugh at myself to shame.
I do not regret the funny phases
For now, I am a funny and a wise parent.
And of course, a lovable husband!
They ask me how I do it,
To be so happy in this lovely cottage.
Well, I smile as I close the chapter
And said, "I lived everyday as the main character."

3. The one week fairytale

I had every reason to leave,
Yet I stayed.
I had every right to
Not take that risk,
Yet I did.
I let myself believe in you
All over again.
I let myself immerse in your
Idea of love.
Little did I know,
It would only be
A one-week fairytale.
The sudden switch
From a blush to a frown,
Had really brought me down.
I never thought that I would be able to count
The days of our perfect fairytale.
Just when I allowed my feelings to grow,
You nipped them in the bud
As though you did not sow.
I tried to defend you
And tried to blend in,
But my fragile heart

Decided to put that to an end.
I will never forget
The seven glorious days,
For I learned how to love,
But sadly, I had to cry.
For I saved it for you,
Hence I was undervalued.
I knew that I could not go on for long,
To doubt and to be doubted upon,
I had to end the sleepless nights
By thinking rationally once again.
Thank you, my love
For that fairytale.
You were my first,
But sadly would not be my last.
These words are how I exactly feel,
Because just when I started to heal,
You completely cut off the zeal.
For now, I really have to go
To achieve new heights
And make myself light
From the heavy things in my heart, per se.
You left a void
That shattered me,
I now have you
Only in my memory.
And if you ever think of me,

Always remember that
I held on to you,
But you let me go.

4. Unsafe haven

I lost my safe haven,
The place I felt seen
Even in my quirky tees;
The place I felt happy
Even when there was nothing to eat;
The place I held on too tight
That perhaps, it struggled to survive.
I tried to water my green grass
To make it grow,
Its health dwindled instead!
I was taken aback
By its sudden unhealthy sprouting,
Little did I know
That I fed it too much.
I called it my home,
My comfort and strength,
That I forgot to give it space,
Whereby, I never left.

My constant fondness of it,
Came off repulsive.
It shattered me!
My home could barely live,

Because of me.
I never agreed to see
The reality of it,
For my life would be hopeless
If I could not run to my home
Whenever I needed it.
Until it creaked!
It was about to crumble,
That I realised,
I was making a mess.

I had to run away from it,
To save it from dying,
I had two choices,
And I chose to let it live.
I chose to be homeless,
Only to let my home feel alive once again.

I always felt like I belonged,
I did not know that
The foundation was not strong.
My home shook at mild tremors
And it was going to harm us both instead.

It haunts me to know
That what was once my safe place
Is now not welcoming me anymore,

For I harmed its existence.

5. Questions

Why is it so hard for me to comprehend things?
But not that hard to compliment things?
Am I for real or am I a wreck?
That is where I need to check!
Do I need therapy or do I need to be free?
Is this a phase?
Or is this my place?
Do I follow?
Or do I go?
Do I stay?
Or do I pray?
What if I dream of comfort?
What if I actually have no support?
Do I breathe?
Or do I sleep?
I need rest,
But more so, zest!
Lately, I feel so less,
When I always know, I am not the best.
Am I lost?
Or do I not want to be found?
I need to take a step;
But, all I see is too much depth.

Maybe, I never want to be in debt
And always want to be fed
With surety
To eternity.

6. Utopian

Throughout my life,
I choose you.
I choose you
To be the only one
Who would receive my whole heart.
I choose you amid the chaos.
I choose you as my comforter.
Even though life has its ways
Where we cannot have things our way,
I choose you
To be my one and only.

I would choose you when I age,
Even though you will never be able to contemplate.
I choose to only love once,
To see you happy
Even if you are not with me.
I choose you because
Even amid the storm
The thought of you
Fulfills my heart.
I do not know where you will go
Or where you will be;

At least, I know
In my heart,
There you will be.

7. Repelled

You were a sapio,
But I made you dumb.
You were Sirius
But made me dim.
We were like-forces
And we repelled.
In a world of no physics,
We would be perfect.
We live in a world
Where we cancel
Each other,
The more
We want to be together.

"What could have been?"
Is what we are made for.
We seemed perfect,
But perfect is
Not for this world.

Our fairytale was
Within numbered days,
Our fairytale tale was enough

To make us both
Go insane.

We gave each other our best,
But all we could create
Was a big, big mess.

We are finally separated now
I bet you are having peace
More than ever.

It is cruel!
With you,
I could give my all.
But, cruel is for this world.

Maybe we were meant to shine,
But not together.
Maybe we were meant to grow,
But not together.
We were made for
The most ecstatic,
Shortest fairytale ever.

I will never regret though,

We both intersected our
Parallel lines,
To be with each other.

Maybe we are two different stars,
Shining in the same sky,
Appreciating each other's
Glimmer;
But far away from
Each other.

8. Twisted

Ever seen a perfect face?
That would always invite a gaze,
No matter how unaware,
One gets inevitable glares.

I might have seen in movie screens,
Always with happy scenes.
I have seen a real life perfect face though,
Whose smile is rarely to be seen.

What lies behind those subtle grins?
From where shall one even begin?
The story of the sad pretty eyes
Or the story of the unforeseen goodbyes!

The grand exterior that we see
Who is always clad in burberry,
Standing out amidst the sea
Of unfocused wannabes.
But when will he become aware?
That he is what everyone desires to be.

The sad, lonely eyes tell a different story,

I do not want to believe it,
But, I could see that they harbour anxiety.
Little do they know that
The facade that everyone sees,
Is what has stolen his peace.

9. Breakup

"It is just a breakup," they say,
But she still cannot contemplate it.
"You will get over it," they say,
It has been eight months and her heart is still in pain.
She is living her deepest fears,
But no one could hear,
Her silent cries
And silent screams
Begging to be seen.
She is at a point where she needs to heal,
But to her, that would mean accepting reality.
A reality where she did not only lose her lover,
But her best friend as well.

She looks for him in the unfamiliar faces
And clings onto the hope that
He is somewhere out there
Remembering his promises.
This poor lady kept hers,
Thinking it is him every time her phone rings.

He never reached out,
He could have moved on,

While she is yet to realise
That he is not the one.
She thinks he needs space;
While all she needs to realise
Is that she needs to breakaway.

10. Lest I forget

Many derive inspiration from sunny days,
But I, from starry nights!
The light years which are inexplicably magical,
Could rekindle the happy times in my mind today.
The stars that shone back then,
Are manifesting those beautiful memories
In the sky today,
In the most beautiful kind of way!
Among the sea of stars,
There is a Sirius!
And I, a dreamy being,
Had personified Sirius!
And I, a skeptic being,
Had found a human Sirius!
Who would never be aware
Of this analogy and my cosmic craze.
I, a passionate star-lover,
I, an avid star-gazer,
Would go all in for star-like creatures!
For to me, an ordinary being,
Such are far beyond my reach.
Lo! This world works in mysterious ways,
For I, the ordinary being

Who gets intimidated by personified constellations,
Lest I forget!
That I was also created,
By the creator of stars
In the most beautiful kind of way!

11. Forbidden Love

Timing,
And that was it.
You were just passing by
The corridors,
And I flipped.

Talking,
And we Clicked!
With the sound of the clock,
Tik-tok-tik.

Charming?
Beyond imagination,
But, this forbidden love
Is beyond my contemplation.

Love,
It exists.
But, painfully
In my memory.

12. Silly fantasy

So my whole world crumbles!
I wish that I had at least
Feared for this day,
But, I never did.

In my mind, you would be there till my dying day,
And I trusted it.
I would see you wait for me
As I walk down the aisle,
In my dreams.

Seeing a day, where you are no longer mine
Never crossed my mind,
And now it is here.
I am in pieces,
I could hear myself break
In the harshest kind of way.
No glass could shatter
Even with all the force
The same way my heart did.
I lost my dream
At 23,
And nothing shatters a man more

Than the inability to dream.

The heart manifesting as a glass,
So beautifully adorned by your warmth,
Is now all over the place,
Losing its form.

My happiness manifests itself
In the form of a bird.
Flying away beyond yonder,
And never to come again.
Your were that happiness of mine,
And to you, I was your cage.
And setting you free,
Means setting my happiness free from me
To eternity.
But certain things are just not meant to be.

I still long for you
Like I always did,
I still dream of your
Heavenly kiss.

My love, you were
My home
And now, I am homeless
And dilapidated,

I am basically a refugee.

Of course,
I wish you well,
I want to see you soar,
I want to see you live,
To see you smile, laugh
And be happy
Even if it is not with me.

But, I cannot lie
That I still long,
And I still wish
To hear you say:
That you love me,
And that is my silly fantasy.

13. The Storm cloaked in a warm summer breeze

The calmest they had ever seen,
Sheltering the turmoil underneath.
The endless smiles they all adore,
Protecting the endless frowns that are unseen.
The exuberant, happy aroma they follow,
Covers the spiralled thoughts with a deep hollow.
The vivacity that catches everyone's attention,
Cloaks the chaos in the other dimension.
The soul that dries the tears of others,
Needs to dry its midnight tears more than ever.
The soul is nothing but a storm,
Cloaked in a warm summer breeze.

14. Star

The star which I see tonight,
Behind that cloudy shadow;
Is light years away from
The dreamy days,
The hopeful days,
The happy days.

I wonder if I could capture that star,
And travel through time,
To the fine yesteryears.
But the only way I could capture it
Is through my blurry lens,
To frame it.

I was not born a star,
But I was born to love one.
I was not born with courage,
But I am strong in those arms.
The captured star
Resides in my heart, but controls my mind,
For when I fail to give it peace,
It stirs trouble in me.

I plan to treasure this star
For as long as I live;
To carry it everywhere
No matter the distance or time.
The sands, the seas,
Can never stop me
From loving my star
To death and even beyond infinity.

15. Las

You were the bubbly one,
You were known for exuding positivity,
You never said no to tea,
You were always there for me.
You are now a complain box,
You have become so angry,
You get triggered easily,
And I wonder, "what could it be?"

Why have you left yourself?
What have you done to the old you?
Is there something that is bothering you?
Or is there some excruciating pain
Behind those beady eyes,
Those half crooked smiles?
What are you so worried about?
If it helps, just shout!
Shout out your questions,
Shout out your answers.
And seek for help
Or seek for your old self.

What made you this way?

Well, that would not be easy to say.
Did you remove the walls?
The walls that guard
The place that gives you the lubb dubb sound.
Oh no, have you removed all your guards?
Is there nothing left?
You rented out that place for some guest, I heard.
But no, you have given the guest free rent
Permanently, instead!
Oh, Happy Las,
Where have you gone?
Are you going to be like this forever?

Why did you not keep a few guards?
Why did you tear all the walls?
They say that you thought that you were granted protection,
But now, all you face is brutal rejection.
Seek for your old self, my las.
Take back your place.
A place where you can be the bubbly las again,
No more tears, no more waits,
And no more excruciating pain.

Grow stronger, my Las.
The guest is not guarding your place that well,
And it has been seen that the door is randomly left opened.
Your place is now exuding negativity,

No more laughter or joy,
But a place of sadness and pain.
Your guest is not watering the plants,
They are dead, I heard.
There are no more greens,
Your place is now a stinking hole,
You need to save it before it gets too old.

Revamp your place,
Tame your lubb dubb sound once again,
And try to win back your place
And make it safe.
My Las, you can!
You are strong,
You are bold,
A warrant is what you need;
To write for the guest
And conquer your old self, once again.

16. Regrets?

I imagine myself visitng a museum,
Displaying the different phases of my life.
I imagine myself gliding along a mirrored shelf,
Displaying the different perceptions from each phase.
I smile and laugh at certain things,
Until I reached the shelf,
Displaying cringe-worthy things.
I wonder if I could live without regrets,
To understand the depth,
And be empathetic towards the version of myself
Who made certain decisions.
I stop by a corner where I could see
Why I thought that he was worthy;
Yes, I was deceived, but I really did not see!
I start to negotiate for that version of me instead.
I move towards a bigger shelf to glance
At the times that I did not want to eat;
Should I hate that version of me? No!
I should embrace it instead.
I made mistakes here and there,
I see regrets everywhere!
I suddenly stop by a shelf which beautifully diplays,
The version of me that could perceive things maturely.

Alas! I do away with all regrets,
For the state that I am in,
Tells me that I am perfectly fine,
For every version of me did blend in well,
At every particular point of time.
I start embracing all the phases of my past,
Even the phase that shattered me,
Only for me to be unbreakable today;
So, just leave it to be that way;
For time and place have always been connected,
And that is perfectly okay,
We ought to live that way.
For in the end,
What is meant for me,
Will surely come my way.

17. Dormant

Maybe memories are enough to make us carry on in life.
Well, I would not have it any other way:
The little infinities,
The laughter,
Are etched as means to make me live.
They pump into my heart,
For my heart needs them
To make me carry on,
The same way it needs blood.
But, from all the memories,
The one which will help me live the most,
Is knowing that I was once someone
Whom you loved the most.
I once was yours and you were mine,
For each passing second.
I once called you mine;
And that will surely heal my mind.

18. The Void

The well lit room
Suddenly feels empty;
It is not a heartbreak,
Nor some stolen peace.
It is just a void
That fills the room,
Echoing the melody
Of a lonely moon.

It is not a sad story,
It does not need the word sorry.
It is nothing bad,
It is nothing sad,
It is just the void
That fills the room.
The mystic void
That creeps into the heart,
The ecstatic poet
Suddenly breaks apart.
It is nothing serious,
It is no one's fault.
It only makes one subtly furious
Or at best, a little dull.

It is the void that a lover leaves
In one's chaotic heart,
For the lover is a thief
Who steals from this independent Las;
Her long lost happy nights
Without having to wait for someone
To say goodnight.
The lover never intended on making
Her feel this way,
He would always know what to say
The next day.

It is not his fault,
It never was and
Never will be.
It is just that he fails to see
The void that he leaves
In his lover's heart
Whenever they have to part.

19. Wake Up

He is thriving,
While I stare blankly at the ceiling.
He sleeps,
I cannot breathe.
He needed a break,
And now my heart aches.

I desire to loathe him,
I desire to set him free,
But it just cannot be.
I need to hate him,
I need to set him free,
But I cannot hate him,
I still wish he is my destiny.

While he scurries through lanes,
And follows his dreams,
I feel an excruciating pain;
Thinking, "What if he forgets about me?"

I fail to acknowledge
That this is the end,

I search for reasons
To defend his decision.
Well, I am a fool
I have become so uncool.
What if I see him someday?
Living our dreams;
But just not with me.

20. Mundane Class

Dreary is what I feel,
This is not where I want to be,
Exposed to things I had never seen.
Dumbstruck! I wish to be where I want to be.
Gloom is what I see,
It is late, it is dark,
There is no more spark.
The noise is bad
Especially when you are sad;
I will be free,
And finally see what life is
Without anxiety.
I wish to understand whatever I am hearing;
For whatever this is,
It will have a bearing;
On me, who is yet to see
Reality without anxiety!
Coercion is bad,
It can make a person go mad,
I am already there,
I just have to not care;
So I can always bear
More mundane classes,

That academic life is yet to bring.

21. Acceptance

I was his world, he said,
While my own was crumbling.
I was whom he was willing to love
At one hundred percent while I did at one!
He held on to me
Amidst my anxiety.
He reassured
When I was not even sure;
Of myself or anybody else.
He was such a sweet melody.
He called me queen
Even when I was not keen of me.
He loved me
With so much zeal!
I remember him,
He is such a sweet, sweet memory.

I do not know how it stopped,
But it did.
And I knew long before he did,
With my premonition,
Though I still dread the contemplation,
I knew that he let me go

And I went with the flow.
And now I have one big hole,
In my heart of hearts,
Trying to comprehend
How some endings
Could be great starts;
When everything is falling apart!
The only thing I could do now,
Is fret over as well as glorify the past.

22. The Gentleman

Unaware, I was
When he made a stop.
All I could hear was
The sound of the thundering halt!
And suddenly, I see something green,
"It is the Ninja bike green," they say,
Whereby the colourblind me could not see.

Behind my specs, I squinted my eyes,
Only to see a pair of dashing blue eyes,
Signalling something to me instead!
It was the most blasé thing, he said,
But my heart raced;
And it was a thousand beats per minute, I almost fled.
Telling myself,
"Oh, how entertaining, a roadside dhaba can be!"
He made his way to my table
And said,
"Can I borrow this chair to your left?"
And there I realised,
It was the gentleman from the block.
And I felt nothing but shocked.
Clad in a biker suit,

Unnoticeable he was,
When all he ever did
Was being green,
The Greenest flag of all;
Contrary to the red ones of my past,
Whereby my colourblind eyes could clearly see.

The gentleman in a biker suit,
Was something I never thought I would see.
Well, I wondered
What he truly ought to be!

23. Our Last

You whispered,
"I love you"
Amidst the bustling streets,
Before we parted.
And I just smiled,
Taking everything for granted,
Looking forward to
Our next date.

Little did I know
That there would never be
A next date.
"I hate you,"
I said.
"But I have to,"
You said.

Numbness took hold of me,
Was it because of dumbness
Or carelessness?
Ong thing I know,
I was flabbergasted.
"We were so in love,"

I said.
"Think about my circumstances,"
You retorted.
"What about my feelings?"
I fret.
"You will be alright,
And I wish you the best."

How can this be?
You were never ready
To lose me.
And now
You are Setting me free.
"I do not want to,"
You said.
"But I have to,"
You added.

I wake up,
Wishing we spent more time
The last time we met.
If only I had known
It was our last time
Being lovers,
When we cared less about others.
If only I hugged you,
If only I had told you,

That you were
My Sirius.

I wish that things would change,
I think of your warmth
Only to realise
That I have been feeling cold, ever since I knew
That I would not grow old with you.
As helpless as I can be,
Knowing that you cannot be with me;
One thing I can live by,
Is knowing you are somewhere out there,
Healthy and alive.

24. Do not

Sometimes you make somebody your home
But sadly, you are not theirs.
Your number one priority
Would not even make himself free
For you.
Your hurt
Comes off as an act,
While you feel the pangs
As though you are getting a heart attack.

Your sleepless nights
Are their delight.
You write paragraphs
Only to be seen.

The tears dripping
On the paragraphs you wrote,
Are nothing but their funny oath.

Do not treat someone
Like your oxygen,
For when they leave,
You may not be able to breathe again.

Hence, set yourself free,
And be your own number one priority.

25. Circa 2017, a.

Picturing you with some other girl
Is torturous to one's mind,
Body and soul.
This poem should not be written,
But it is an ode to an irresistible you!
Tall guys are cute,
And so are you!
It should not be written.
But, it already half-written.
Okay, the eyes are cute,
The hair is messy,
The attitude is inexplicably charming
And now the poem that should not be written,
Has actually come to an end!

26. My world

Tender love,
From them who gave me life;
Sacrificial love,
From them who let me be.
Growing up,
They gave me priceless memories,
I hope they know
That they are the best, to me.
The warmth they provide in my misery,
The smile they wear when they see me happy,
How did I get to be this lucky?
Oh Lord, they are the best thing to me.
The sleepless nights to keep me safe,
The endless lessons to make me brave,
I am who I am today,
Because of them, who gave me life.
Perhaps, there is another universe,
I sincerely wish
To still be their daughter
Out there.

27. Circa 2017, b.

He is the one I would call my own,
He, who was clearly brought up by kind angels.
He seems like the one that I had asked for,
Through prayers, and all I had to do, was be patient.
He is the one who gives me smiles,
When life feels a little unfair,
And gives me butterflies
With his flirty stares.
He gives me hope to enjoy a life
Which is worth our hardwork and strife.
He shows a sweet and shy love at first,
But his eyes scream, "sincerity!"
I would often thing that this would end,
But he ends up being sweeter by the day.
My major flaws seem non-existent to him,
My capabilities became clearer since I met him.
I know not, yet,
If he and I are meant to be,
But all I know is that,
He gave me the sweetest high school memories.
Those little cherished moments,
Through stolen glances and wonderful conversations,
Were the reason behind my lob-sided smiles.

His kind, dreamy eyes and his gentleman behaviour,
Could be my answered prayers.
He is a gentleman with roots,
Who takes his responsibilities seriously,
And most importantly to me,
He has been taught to treat a girl so sweetly.
How grateful I am,
To the ones who gave him life,
For, they raised such a fine gentleman,
The best thing that ever happened to me.

28. State Of Misery

Candlelight dinners,
Romantic they can be,
Here we are,
Getting them for free.

Broadway shows:
Incomparable
To the plays we get to see
Every day, for free.

Luxury;
Is all we see,
We do not need employability.

Enlightenment so fine;
That education could make us blind.

A lit up town;
A facade for people who are feeling down,
Covering the darkness
Underneath.

Oh, you and me,
In this state of misery!
Where starvation and corruption
Are accessories.

29. The Silent Room

I could not even recognise myself anymore;
I was a broken vessel,
Broken to tiny pieces.
My heart felt numb,
I was getting dumber
Day by Day.

I cried in the silent room,
Away from the common din,
And my life was dim.
Days go by in the silent room,
My life was getting worse,
And worldly things made me
Question my worth.

One fine day,
He touched my heart
One fine day,
I felt His presence.
I felt him embracing the broken me
He said, "Child, You are safe with me."

He saved me,

He fixed me,
He made me whole.
I do not need anything else in this world
But, His Presence.

He took me places I never thought I would see,
He made me brave,
More than I could ever be.
He renews my strength every morning,
And He is all I need.

Now, days are getting brighter,
He comforts me in the storm.
He makes me strong,
But the best of all,
I feel His presence, through it all.

His love is beyond my comprehension,
He loves a broken vessel like me,
He saved me.
Life with Him
Is the greatest blessing of all.
He is my King,
My everything.
To Him, I am enough,
To Him, I am a prized possession.

To Him, I am strong;
No more fears,
No more tears.
Jesus, you teach me
To live my life
So beautifully.
You are all I need.

www.ingramcontent.com/pod-product-compliance
Lightning Source LLC
La Vergne TN
LVHW090132160826
845673LV00017B/2436
9798892770040